Ridin' the Moon in Texas

BOOKS BY NTOZAKE SHANGE

THEATRE
*for colored girls who have considered suicide/when the
rainbow is enuf*
Three Pieces

POETRY
nappy edges
A Daughter's Geography

FICTION
Sassafrass, Cypress & Indigo
Betsey Brown

Ridin' the Moon in Texas

Word Paintings

Ntozake Shange

St. Martin's Press / New York

RIDIN' THE MOON IN TEXAS. Copyright © 1987 by Ntozake Shange. All rights
reserved. Printed in the United States of America. No part of this book may be
used or reproduced in any manner whatsoever without written permission
except in the case of brief quotations embodied in critical articles or reviews.
For information, address St. Martin's Press, 175 Fifth Avenue, New York,
N.Y. 10010.

Design by Andy Carpenter

Library of Congress Cataloging in Publication Data

Shange, Ntozake.
    Ridin' the moon in Texas.

    I. Title.
PS3569.H3324R5   1987   811'.54   86-26278
ISBN 0-312-88929-1

First Edition
10 9 8 7 6 5 4 3 2 1

This book is dedicated to
Vickie Miller & Ana Mendieta
whose lives inspired me &
whose murders haunt me & the earth.

Contents

Acknowledgments

I want to thank each and every
visual artist with whom I was
in contact during the experience
of writing this book. I especially
want to thank those who
introduced me to the work of
artists unknown to me: Rozlyn
Allen, Esther de Veschy, Marilyn
Lubetkin, and Fletcher Mackey. Once again
I must thank my editor,
Michael Denneny, for believing
in me.

A Note to the Reader

The Evolution of Ridin' the Moon in Texas

My father was a painter, before he became a surgeon.
While he was a surgeon, there was this strange room in our
house in St. Louis called a "dark room." I don't quite know
what that meant to me, but I knew images leapt out of his
hands at all hours of the day and night, whenever he opened
that door. I saw color and I saw a story. I saw a face and
knew a lifetime. These imaginative visual sweeps were
courted by my mother's consistent and reverent readings of
Dunbar, Shakespeare, Cullen, and Hughes, whose images
were tactile and three-dimensional for me: love, the crystal
stair, the rivers.

As I grew I surrounded myself with images, abstractions
that drew warmth from me or wrapped me in loveliness. In
moments of courage, I'd converge with some violent politi-
cal works or what Wopo Holup and I have termed "the ugly
paintings," because as a writer I knew that all that is seen
consciously or cognitively is not beautiful, but valuable.
Loving someone to me, at one point, meant enveloping
them in beauty: smells, visions, textures, me. Later I discov-
ered that one must challenge in loving as in life. Challenge
one's intimate to see, not as I see, but what I see.

The notion to begin this book, a collection of prose and
poetry based solely on the work of visual artists, came to me
in my dream sleep where I see most pungently and richly.
I'd moved from the Lower West Side of Manhattan to make
my home in Houston, yet I wandered Texas as a blind
woman. I saw, but could not make a connection. I touched,
but felt unmoved. I dug soil, looking for roots, finding none.
I said to myself maybe my spirits are telling me I'm still in
New York skipping around Soho or 57th Street. This I re-
jected immediately. If I was anywhere besides Texas, I was
roaming the paintings and installations of artists around the
country whose work fed me the nonverbal ambrosia word-
users hunger for. I was hankering for communion with a

community I'd lost, for dreams and visions I couldn't just fly up to. I asked a number of artists, some of whom were friends, others unknown to me, if they would allow me to create a verbal dialogue with their works, finding, seeking out what a poet might find in a tapestry or a sculpture, or a watercolor. Paintings and poems are moments, capturing or seducing us, when we are so vulnerable. These images are metaphors. This is my life, how I see and, therefore, am able to speak. Praise the spirits and the stars that there are others among us who allow us visions that we may converse with one another. *Ridin' the Moon in Texas* allowed me this remarkable privilege.

ntozake shange
Houston, Texas
April 24, 1986

Un tiro 22
que sale
desde el primer corazón tortuado
dá en el blanco
dá en el blanco
es mas certero que las balas
disparadas sin amor
sin odio
es más certero que las balas
disparadas sin amor
sin odio
> —Carlos Mejta Godoy,
> "Un Tiro 22 de Guitarra Armada,"
> *Guitarra Armada*

I start pulling my guts out,
those red silk cords
spiraling skyward,
and I'm climbing them
past the moon and the sun
past darkness
into white.
I mean to live.
> —Ai Ogawa,
> "Nothing But Color,"
> *Killing Floor*

As you step on the edge of my doubting,
you're free.
> —A.R.C. Finch,
> *The Mermaid Tragedy*

Ridin'
the
Moon
in
Texas

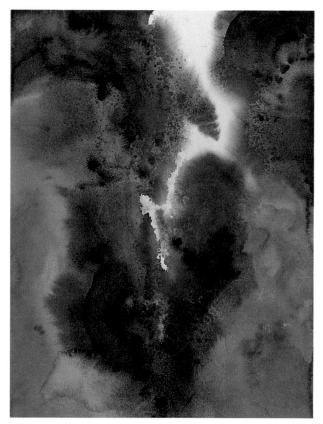

Laura Caghan, "Night Lightning," Watercolor, 30″ x 22″

Prologue: Night Lightning

Hurricanes rattle the house, pull up trees, send roofs crashing down upon flower vases, children and the candles they tell us to keep. The rain assaults the fire of the burning candles / leaves us in darkness / shaken, trembling in the wind / the water slowly inching through the floors / til the arches of our feet are damp & wet. Hurricanes are part of life in East Texas / that's where I live here in tornado watch, flood watch, hurricane watch, Houston, Texas.

Night lightning is sometimes all we can depend on to see. Leaving New York was like a hurricane for me. I was thrown, whisked away like Dorothy for a need for "home." Here, I have one, night lightning & all. Yet, the joy of seeing what New York can be, what New Yorkers can create was gone. The delight & questioning that visual artists across the country offered me was gone.

I drew. I built. I painted. I danced. These, like writing, are solitary affairs, not impromptu salons in the Quarter, Soho, or North Beach. *Ridin' the Moon* came to me thanks to the understanding of so many artists, some of whom I've never met but who were willing to share my need to see. They understand I live in a hurricane zone: everything might disappear.

I speak to these sculptures, wood prints, and paintings as I would to a friend over coffee or champagne. *Ridin' the Moon* is not an explanation of a visual maze, but a conversation that goes on all night long, when the house shakes & the lights go out. I remember vaguely, but intimately, a Mapplethorpe nude, a Pindell tapestry, a Conwill pyramid, a Puryear ellipse. I remember & then I can go on & speak my mind. Reminding my friends of the beauty of "Night Lightning": the glory of the discourse of seeing.

Oh, thunder & lightning is not the devil beating his wife, it's the sky bleeding flowers.

Patricia Ollison Jerrols, "Ridin' the Moon in Texas," Photograph

Ridin' the Moon in Texas

Houston Rodeo & Livestock Show ain't never seen the same since we come riding in from Arcola. All colored and correct. Long-sleeved shirts, cowboy hats, chaps, spurs, covered wagons, and a place all our own in Memorial Park. Ain't never seen that many niggahs in Memorial Park no way, least not at 4:30 in the morning. Perking coffee over open fires and warming each other with bourbon and one rodeo yarn after another. Ain't nothing white folks can do bout it, even Sam Houston enlisted this black fella could talk five Indian languages—five and English, of course. Even Sam Houston had enough sense to ask this niggah to go talk some sense to them Cherokees, so's they wouldn't fight gainst Texas independence. Well, we independent now and riding proud right down Hwy. 59 to Texas Avenue. Don't understand why that woman didn't buy those boys some hats. She knows cain't no man be in a trailride or a rodeo without a hat. Shame, too. They came all the way from Abilene to sit by the wayside with them other folks. Just looking. And I'll say one thing. That flock of niggahs on them gorgeous horses and them wagons, now that was something to look at! Must be why ain't none of us forget it. The trailride and all. And the rodeos. The black ones, of course, white folks don't quite have the hang of it. I mean, how you sposed to look, your image, on your horse. It takes a colored point of view.

"Twanda, whatcha gone do tonight? Louisiana Red is up for everything from bronc-busting to steel-dogging!"

"Oh go on, gal, you know I cain't do nothing but barrel racing. Sides, I've got some business out yonder."

"Whatchu mean, you got some business out yonder? You ain't plannin' on messin' with me or them hard-head cowboys come to laugh at us tonight. You know this is our night, the All-Women's Rodeo, Navasota, Texas, honey.

We the stars this evening, girl, even if you do gotta itch in your twat—them races come first—you got some business out yonder—huh!—you better check Dallas—you really gonna let that Jamaican chick use your horse for calf-roping?"

"Her horse is sick. She's an allright broad. You know she was champion two years in a row."

"But not with your horse."

"You know you can be one petty bitch when you wanna."

"I spose that's why you gonna investigate your business out yonder?"

"Listen, honey, I'ma see about Dallas. He misses me if I'm gone more than a hour and before a race he just gets beside himself and I gotta sweet talk him and snuggle up to him, specially fore I put that bridle thru his mouth—he don't like that thing at all—I sure do like them Oak Ridge Boys. Listen, can't ya hear it?"

"Hell, no. Why don't cha just ride bare back."

"I might—"

"Sure."

"No, I might saunter thru the night bare back on Dallas; naked as a jay bird."

"Oh yeah, where?"

"Out yonder, I told ya."

"Girl, you know you don't make no sense sometimes. Did you pay up for the bronc-busting and barrel racing?"

"Course I did. Cost me seventy dollars. That's why I gotta get Dallas feeling high and sweet. We gotta win alla that money back and then some."

"You signed up for the breakaway?"

"Hell, no. That ain't no rodeo.That's some real bullshit. Can you rope a runaway calf?"

"Some folks cain't."

"Well, that ain't shit to me. Rope the damn thing and tie it in eight seconds. That I can understand. Breakaways just some other way for the 'pro-mo-tors' to make some more dough."

"So what? There's money in it."

"And a lotta fools, too."

"Go on now. See bout Dallas. I'ma get me a beer and some barbecue. Thank God, they finally playing Charlie Pride. I just love how that man can sing. Love me some Charlie Pride."

The night was fresh, more like morning should be. The grass and brush beyond the rodeo arena were moist and seductive, begging to be touched or lain on. The moon sat up in the sky like a hussy in red with her legs wide open. So what if all the women riders from Muskogee to Lubbock, Marshall to Lafayette, showed for the All-Women's Rodeo? Just last year, Susie Louise won bronc-busting and she was four months pregnant. Her momma won calf-roping and her daughter ran away with the steel-dogging. Shit. What a night that was. Take a look at those men come to look at us. I can't believe Lee Andrew had the nerve to tell me he came out here cuz he likes to see the expression on my face: see me change from pretty to ugly. Talk about nerve. I'ma bring me one of my pretty cowboys right on back here. It's so quiet. Most like there wasn't no rodeo going on. Maybe I'll ride Dallas by that rhiney boy with those dogging arms, the one in the black and red satin shirt with white fringe and red suede chaps dangling silver coins. He's the one whispered "I'm a black man who wants to ride off on a filly." Yeah, mister. I got something for your ass. God, I wonder how James is doing? I forgot to call the hospital once the ambulance carried him off. That bull stamped all over his ass and he ain't but so big. Big as a minute actually. Not much bigger than a minute. Jesus. That gore was more than I could handle. And that fool Joe-Man had the gall to say I didn't have no heart cuz I was paying up for calf-roping instead of seeing to James. Shit. James finished his event. How was I gonna calf-rope and see to James. Humph. That's awright, Dallas. We're just warming up, that's all. Getting a feel for the wind and the ground round here. Come on, I'ma kick it up! See if we can get neath these tree limbs and over that stream without hurtin' ourselves. Whatchu say, baby? That's a boy. Do like momma say and she'll give you a bright shiny apple. That's a boy. Let's get it. Go for it. There ain't nothing out here but prairie and me and you and the wind. So that makes it the moon, the wind and a little satisfaction. Those folks crazy now, they playing Otis Redding. Come on, now. Show momma whatcha can do. She needs some satisfaction too. Right, baby? Do it for momma.

"Breakaway:

"Nancy Bourdan—Houston—Score 57.

"Sally Johnson—Midnight, Mississippi—Score 55.

"Molly Hanks—Conroe, Texas—Score 52."

"No, man, just give me a beer from that cooler in your truck. I ain't out here to compete tonight. How can I do that? This a All-Women's Rodeo—ain't it? Well, ain't it?"

"Yeah, that why I'm out here, cain't really tell if a woman's a woman til you see how she could ride a horse."

"You right bout that, bro!"

"Gimme that beer and a joint."

"I'ma get some more barbecue but I'ma say one thing. Just one thing. The ladies is the horses. If you get my meaning. But the way my lady friend ride is fantastic. All that tension and excitement from the Diamond L all the way out here to Navasota or Madisonville. Now they got some great rodeo in Madisonville, but you know I got three daughters and I'ma black man and I'd rather have my girls here than anywhere else."

"Oh, man, go and get the barbecue."

"Whatever you say, Bubba. Watch the horses all right. These gals ain't got no more scruples than that white bitch, whatcha call it, Belle Starr?"

"Yeah, man. I got it covered. Just get the beer, man, and let me know if you see that sassy gal what races barrels."

"There's Bo-Beep with those damned armadillos in a pond of draft beer. When these guys gonna learn armadillos get drunk. They chasing beer. They ain't racing. That's all right, Dallas. We'll just ignore that. Okay, baby."

"Hey, Twanda."

"Huh?"

"Ain't that what they call you, Twanda?"

"Some do, some don't. What's it to you?"

"That's a nice-looking animal you got there."

"I know that. You got a nice-looking face too."

"It's just a cowboy's face."

"I know that. Come on, Dallas."

"Hey, don't ride off like that."

"Whatcha think I'm on a horse for, to stay still somewhere? Let's go, Dallas."

"All right, everybody, clear the arena—it's time for the Cotton-eyed Joe."

"Well, cain't you dance, gal?"

"Whatchu mean? Of course I can!"

"Twan, let's me and you gone and do the Cotton-eyed Joe."

"Shit yeah. If you can keep up with me."

"Watch me, baby. Careful how you do that horse and you'll see what all I could do. What all I could do for you, baby."

"Sure, hot stuff."

"Calf-Roping:

"Agnes Moralez—San Antonio, Texas—Score 7.6.

"Sally Johnson—Midnight, Mississippi—Score 8.1.

"Louisiana Red—Lafayette, Louisiana—Score 7.2."

I cain't exactly explain how it happened, but out there somewhere how the prairie snapped up the last bits of night. Bubba and Twanda raced free as sepia roses on their horses' bare back. Holding the manes and each other the way you'd have to when you're dealing with a steer and you come out grinning and then be screaming. They fell out near a smooth mossy cloud neath a cypress tree. "Guantanamera" blasting from the arena.

Guantanamera, Gaujiro, Guantanamera.

Twanda was murmuring, "I'm in the rodeo cuz my momma was and my first night out I won ninety dollars just for running round barrels. You cain't beat that, for running round barrels." Bubba somehow quieted her. He was unsettled by her drive. She had to win. She was one with her horse. She had no sense of anything sides speed and her animal, but that was when she was racing. She said. She liked he was a champion. She said, "Look a heah, I'm a champion too," when she wrapped that huge silver buckle round her slight waist. The hairs from her thighs creeping like ferns from her navel. Women and horses. Black women and horses. An all-women's rodeo. What next? Bubba slapped his thigh and reached for that joint and Bud.

Twanda pulled him to her and let him play with a piece of grass she slipped tween his lips. Then she lay back on his shoulder. Let the sky celebrate her victory: Twanda Rochelle Johnson—Barrel-racing—17.5—First Place—$532.

She smiled, contented; remembered that business she'd had out yonder. Out on the prairie where black folks have always felt at home. She pulled the straw outta Bubba's mouth. He didn't know what was happening til she sang a cowgirl's song / sweet & tough / soft and rough:

let me be a chorus of a thousand / tongues
and your lips dance on a new moon / while
Daddy Cool imagines synchopated
niggahfied erotica on Griggs Road
We'll have skimmed the cream off the milky way/made a permanent ellipse by the yet uncharted tail of Halley's

Comet/these tongues and lips make a time step of Bojangles in fast forward/merely slow motion in a sultry dusk/ so natural/is the tone of your chest under the gaze of the wild stallions by the waterfalls, enveloped by scarlet blossoms like a woman's heart/your sweat seeps into my mouth/we sleep/ deep/deep/like in Texas.

"Hey, ain't that the Judds—ain't that something."

"We gone sleep/deep/deep like in Texas."

Arturo Lindsay, "Indigo's Emergency Care for Wounds That Cannot Be Seen," Collage, 10″ x 8″

Conversations With the Ancestors

ancestral messengers/composition 11

they told me to travel toward the sun
to lift my feet from the soil
engage myself to the wind in a dance
called my own/
my legs, wings of lavender & mauve
they carried me to the sun-cave
the light sweet shadows eclipsing our tongues

we spoke of longings/yearnings/the unknown
we spoke in the tongue of the snake
the hoot of the owl
tongues of our ancestors
dancing with the wind

we traverse the sun
fully fired violet beings
directly overhead the sun-cave
lifting me/coaxing my eyes
to see as theirs do

crisp stalking spirits/proud
swirling spirits/my blood

they've made themselves a home here
blood relatives converging
wherever my soul is lurking
telling me   now   yes   now
go to the center of the sun

we are sending sepia stallions
headstrong appaloosas and cypress carriages
to carry you home

ancestral messengers/composition 13

no, señora rodriguez
you cannot bring the goat to the 13th floor
you must get rid of the chickens, too
yes, señora, i understand the
goat's fresh milk is best for the baby
but the goat cannot go on the elevator to the 13th floor

of course i'll catch señorita diaz
& her roosters/i know what's going on in 9c

no, señora rodriguez, i don't know where
your goat can rest/just not in this building
no, it is not all right to go up the stairs
out of the way of the tenants/oh, please, señora
don't try to take the goat to your sister's
house in queens on the e or the f train

it's against the law, señora
how can i tell you the goat is not
against the law/animals are not
against the law/it's just that
living creatures are not welcome here

torso

she didn't know of womanly ways
she didn't see it in herself
she wandered among protea bougainvillea
antheriums birds of paradise
a flower? no, a petal
of a woman not knowing
her fragrance enchanted
men who could not bring themselves
to call her name
all they could do was turn away
their eyes shut tightly
refusing to lose the vision, the scent
of the petal of a woman
the flower meandering
by the hummingbirds

2 march 1984 (cowry shells & heart)

we sing so much of love
we carry walkmans and sony tape recorders
am/fm stations blaring/ even though
our rhythms   our guitar pulses
are prohibited on the subway/ considered déclassé
north of 57th street/ south of gramercy park
our hearts don't beat
they sweep us off our feet
block the chaos & tumult the white people
call civilization/ our love songs
wind gently from smokey's tender lips
or cry out passionate from chaka khan
& celia/ why ruben blades seduced
the empire state building/ you should have seen
her blushing in the twilight
first red then pinkish
her tower tense then giving in to
the sweet refrains of a black man's voice
a capella among the clouds
bluer than b.b.'s moans/ scarlet
in the fashion of la lupe/ more serious
than marley/ more graceful than nat king cole
we sing so much of love
it's our largest industry   our most
marketable product & still
we have not learned the songs of tenderness
that might mend
our broken hearts
cowry shells/ sequin jackets
protect us momentarily
just before we beat the hell out of each other
leaving bloody riffs/ scar tissue keloids
what we call romance

18 march 1984

swing spanish moss men
machetes in hand
cut back the cane the pines & cypress
take back the soil that is our own
the cotton red with blood
rice rotting our legs away

swing spanish moss men
hang languid from those lynching ropes
air/where is there air?
we breathe our deaths so casually
like making morning coffee
the smell so familiar whiffs of it
bring us running downstairs
where ghosts step in single file
over our bodies
hoping we might see anything

swing spanish moss men while I
gather my small parcels/my past
let me tarry on just a little further
before I join you in single file
stepping over our blood kin
still flirting with death
mistaking al jolson for dr. j
let me walk with you just a bit longer
i'm learning to use my machete
in el salvador we use galil machine guns
wage war on death
blossoming despite the tortures
machetes are not always enough

Howardena Pindell, "Three Views of Mt. Fuji," Tempera, gouache, postcards

Three Views of Mt. Fuji

she got her sister to ride wit her to the liquor store / waz most 10:00 awready / wdnt be no more wine till monday / if they misst this. the fog lifted to let her thru. red lights faded as she drew near. her sister waited in the car, chewin gum. shakin her head / melissa's loosin her mind. & she chewed harder.

in the liquor store wit alla these italians talkin bout wounded knee / what'd they know. damned injuns oughtta be glad they aint dead / waznt geronimo dead. & cochise. they looked at melissa as if she waz somethin they know nothin abt / & the heat of their stares ran her out.

two bottles of manishevitz under her arm. she drove home a different way / same as her aunt learned her / to divert attention from her routine / to surprise always a possible attacker by going somewhere / unusual / so they drove way cross town to *the razzmatazz cafe* / a poet's bar / or a bar tended by poets / a poet's enclave / a poet's shadow / somewhere safe to hide / in the bathroom & drink this sweet sweet wine.

carol, the sister, squirmed & made faces. poets were boring & boorish. waz not goin to be a good evening. lotsa hands under the table / shared bottles shared lips & promise never manifest. carol waz not excited / but melissa pulled right into the front of *the razzmatazz* / slammed the door / turned quickly her eyes insistin carol get up / join the soiree.

oh a soiree. a party for an ol beat poet / a reading of works salvaged from his madness / a coterie of possibles stranglin in tap beer / forgotten lovers. sawdust scavengers articulatin remembered ridiculousness / their fathers dyin / lyin clumsily to someone else they loved / maybe a recant of time in the joint or sanatorium / the halfway house / a railroad car / maybe a poem to the women who were impressed & quickly exhausted by the immensity of their idol's appetites for sacrifice: for naomi. bette. diana. lavinia. for . . . / on & on thru the nite. melissa waz recognized by a self-appointed host / who referred to her as a fine poetess / poet-ess / an inconceivable entity / a non-actual manipulator of language / a feminine peculiarity with language / a less than poet / real / thing / a term / like 'lady' or 'mamselle' / a rejoinder to the middle ages / an insult. she refused to read. no one got the point.

one reluctant visionary established a corner as his own. 5 empty chairs surrounded him. a table covered with sheets of paper / presumably poems / piled or twistin / he too did not read. but he wept / when the celebrity of the 50's attempted to shout a poem to the mirror / not recognizin an audience sides himself. this recluse poet / a table of his own / pulled himself together / read the master poet's work from that very spot / & the two of them / the mad one & his counterpart / exchanged looks of tenderness / neither waz familiar with / the hermit champion left abruptly after pullin melissa outta her seat.

melissa knew what waz goin on / he insisted she did not. i didnt call you. he snarled. tuggin her arm up against his chest. I didnt want to see you tonite. he seemed more disappointed than angry / more frightened than fearsome / melissa lingered in the damp of his chest. i wanted to hear some poems. i needed some poems & voices nearby. it's not good to drink alone. & she nodded toward her sister reading *The Daily Life of the Aztecs* under the phone. the poet sighed. so happy she had not said what he knew she meant. she had not declared her love of his being. how she simply wanted to be near him. more importantly she had not said she wanted to know him / like the poems she tossed casually outta her mouth / day after day. the wine. the images / him listening to her murmur worlds.

the ol beat poet had stationed himself atop the bar in mismatched shoes / locks that cda been dreads had he known abt bob marley / swallowed his face. everyone waz afraid for him // he might become a fool more easily now than remain the prophet of the new day he had misst by movin too fast /

goin the wrong way // rememberin too much or forgettin somethin that cd not be forgotten & so wound itself around his spirit / & the more he forgot, the more twisted he became. everyone knew there waz a secret / fetid & angry.

melissa watched all this over the shoulder of her lover / a poet afraid to look at his fate in twenty years / screamin on top of a bar. no ben webster here. this waz not Bird's legacy to be crusted / wantonly inchoate / chucklin about other times / no one cd recall. this poet, holdin melissa. breathin tears & fear on her neck / waz callt smith / & that waz all / just smith.

& he commanded the respect of the locals & some cross country knew his work. tight. sparse. brutal in the one thrusted-ness of his voice. smith waz perhaps an answer to someone sides lissa / someone's searching in *dead lecturer* / *afrodisia* / *preface to a 20 volume* / *golden sardines.* smith waz the other one / the unassigned specter of our lives / with a vocabulary of earlier days / sensibilities of our times / the mixture of the eras created no followin for him / cept melissa & those souls who had lost a space for themselves in the world / lost the languages of the present & muffled their paucity of connection with morphine / began the conversations with sorrow on a toot of cocaine / a syringe.

smith waz a businessman / a dealer / which hurt him more than watchin the crazy beat actin up / hurt him like discoverin his cousin dead in the tub / drowned in a nod / his buddy hangin from a water pipe in the 2nd basement of a project / hurt him like melissa, show up uncallt for. melissa bein someone he protected from himself, as best he knew / how.

& she refused his good will / his refusal to be / known / as he refused her faith in him. she drank sweet wine down Hwy 101 / as he left / scars lickin in the bronze of his arms. tryin to forget.

carol chewin gum. catchin her history like somebody chasin a cockroach / closed her book. marched outta *the razzmatazz* when the ol beatnik began a high mass for his mother / in fronta the hard whiskey shelves just beyond the bar. she had no time for the recently dead / near dead &

sufferin. she determined her sister, melissa, cd not join this fraternity of sadness / come-uppances & private martyrdom. carol stalked / thru the swingin doors / pullt melissa from smith. lets go home. this aint shit. the niggers are crazy. all yall gone crazy. look like dead folk kissin. & she waz right.

melissa clung to smith / imperceptibly / like somebody passed away. she thot her body thru his blood & caught his cries wit the tip of her tongue. melissa waz not safe. her sister took her home.

melissa drunk / carol angry. the ride from potrero to the ocean musta been like judas' carryin on while christ burdened himself for us all / guilt stifled everythin / fog sat down on the curbs / the ocean spat silver on the beach / carol took melissa's bottle away. he aint no good. damn melissa.

melissa climbed into her bed by the sea / cried a thousand smiths / each one breakin her skin / so she waz bloody & scraped / she rollt in her blood tryin to kiss him / & when he callt / she sounded regular . . . yes / i'll be there. carol hated her. carol watched shanghai lil makin topsy take the weight.

melissa barely made it. she cdnt see / fog & trolly tracks / cop cars & visions of him / she cd hardly make out the corners / but some kinda way she made it down the hill / she sat imaginin smith holdin her / wantin her / finally explainin why / he did her how he did / & she smiled imbecilically / cuz she had lost control / her muscles / her breath / all controlled by somethin else / somethin no good / like smith smilin / smith movin inside her / his beard diggin thru her cheeks / the blood they sucked from each other's flesh / this waz not ordinary / melissa no regular nothin / their embrace cd be murder or a poem / melissa found her way down the street / hills / nothin but hills. here to find smith on top of the hill. where she came from only a river & heavy scents / she took each step like a gift / goin to see the wizard / the body concealin heavens / smith somewhere at the top of this / he grabbed her up / his hair braided a million times / braids fallin from his skull / cheekbones raised to holy angles / his mouth rushin over her / sayin good things / come in. me-lissa. please. come in. i want to see you. melissa. the blood

drippin from his arms / she tried to wipe into her skin / she
rubbed gainst him furiously / & he liked it / pullt round /
pullt away / mad & soft / like uh huh / you dont understand.
melissa / how much i need / melissa kisst his calves / licked
ankles / he went to the typewriter / she moved with his legs
/ her hands & mouth caressin like water / her tongue fol-
lowed his tears down his face.
the poem/ crawled out.

p.s.

he never callt her again. years later he published several vol-
umes of her poems.

Anita Steckel, "Billie Holiday," Montage: Silkscreen and pencil on photograph

Gardenias on the Borderline

imagine this is legal
why it smells like hashish
    i wonder what hashish smells like
       thick vibrant smoke curling /
      a gardenia petal in my palm

my skin might gleam /
    the dark side of the moon
      her voice climbing from my heart
thru the scarred sinews of my throat
a raspy legato / in a colored tone
    minor key
      minority
        needling complacency

i might have a run in my stockin
    but if i go to the ladies room
she might be in there doing whatever
      they say she does / the Daily News
   gossip / "she shoots up"
      she's a shooting star
       crumbling in this smell / is not hashish
     it's old whiskey & rationed lettuce cigarettes

there is no gardenia

    oh yes   please one white gardenia
without one tinge of brown /
   pure cool white &
fragrant at my temple / she is my temple

"where's my will /
what's this strange desire"

i dont want to go back there / now
not there
no song there that taunts me so /
i know i'm not / what
but she must know / i'm not implacable
on purpose / i hurt cleanly
my blood doesn't dry on my skin /
i lick it off
but she must know I feel something / like her
her eyes are meeting mine

"i say i'll move a mountain
& i'll move a mountain"

who does she think she is /

"i say i'll go thru fire
& i'll go thru fire"

doesn't she know who we are /
this isn't real

"i say i'll sail forever
   & i mean forever,
      if i have to hold up the sky"

the colored can't even drink water from the
   same fountain / but
wait / no one's ever given me a gardenia

     "i say i'll care forever
      & i mean forever"

does anyone care for me /
   like all those people enveloped
   by the smoking wilted voice
 of a browning gardenia
maybe i'll smell like this for a while
   i'll let the winter take two steps back
  live gardenias on harvard street in february
no it's not for sale /
   you had to be there /
     listening to billie.

Houston Conwill, "Passages: Earth Space," Site Sculpture, 9' x 9' x 9'

Passages: Earth Space

(for Winnie Mandela and the children of Azania)

there is no one in the bottom of a champagne bottle
there's no guerrilla waiting with loaded uzi
  to sail down the san juan river
    gunning for *commandante zero*
there's no one to help me free nelson mandela
  or bring the *murderers* of victoria mxenge
    to their rightful brutal deaths

the bottom of a champagne bottle is a pitiful
  American gesture / celebrating dishonestly
  the will to die for freedom
    outside durban or capetown

for south african blacks / champagne is *verboten*
  (too good for the dirty kaffirs) *Azanians*

When the ANC marches over botha's
  dried & hate-filled bones / his sinews
  crippled with wickedness / mauled under
  the feet of children whose lives he'd have

wiped out / if it weren't for the mines / diamonds
  & gold / he imagines his skeleton shines
  like gold / his skull on a ray of diamonds /
mind you / he's being crushed as he would
crush angola / as he imagines cabral is silenced /

  botha banned
    the marching feet of millions of children
on their way to free nelson mandela / to
ban krugerrands as the israelis would obliterate
palestines & mengeles /
    no questions asked / only the skin as evidence
  of heinous crimes or innocence /

x-rays of partial plates & root canal work
identify 25,000 dead in el salvador / most of
whom were suffering from plaque & tartar overgrowth
bloody abandoned golf courses & badminton courts
/ twilight leaves their bald bones shimmering
by the roadside

we could be thrashing thru to the enemy /
but this is not a phenomenon of happy hour or
free-basing / this is outside the world of controlled
substances / this is the world of refined deformities
& lush torture / legal starvation & unemployment lotteries

(the more cocaine you do / the longer they can make
you work for them / look at the *Incas* who
are no more / *Machu Picchu* standing vacant
in the shadows of its people / now ghosts)

Maybe sanctions against the dead *Incas* would
prove a mighty tool in the war against nicaragua /
not even the ghosts of the oppressed may cross
the borders of "el otro territorio libre en américa" /
they are after all 'foreign advisors'

between soweto & masaya
are bodies the breadth of the atlantic ocean
bones & spirits mingling with ours / children
of the *Diaspora* / yet we are not rising
to the occasion / not approaching the surface /
our noses hover over mirrors / look we can almost
see our faces between the lines of snow

we are snorting up our senses
our courage is being eaten away by
wine coolers the world senses & raps to roxanne

from the bottom of a champagne bottle
one can only imagine nelson mandela's rage &

wisdom / there are no freedom fighters armed /
& ready / chanting

PATRIA O MUERTE

NICARAGUA VENCIA / EL SALVADOR VENCERA
que viva la liberación de la gente negra
del africa del sur
namibia
angola
grenada
mozambique
quien sabe donde estará / el próximo
territorio libre / no solamente en américa
pero en el mundo /

PATRIA O MUERTE

que viva la liberación mundiale
une vie sans oppression
pour tout / para ti / une vie sans
oppression /
where the color / the color of our
skin is not evidence of heinous
crimes or innocence.

Linda Graetz, "Who Needs a Heart," Acrylic on Canvas, 47½″ x 47½″

Who Needs a Heart

somewhere in soweto there's a small girl
she's brown thin & frightened
she eats cardboard sometimes she's hungry
& she makes believe it's bread & meat
warm meat with butter & salt
tween two slices of bread
she's four years old
she eats grass sometimes she's hungry
cows eat grass so do goats
she thinks she's an animal
there's no one around to hold her
call her name, "Ndekedehe," tell
her a story like rose red & rose white
or maybe someone awready told
her about rose white & so at four
she's decided it's better to be a four-legged creature
than the kind that stand on two legs
with cattle prods & rifles
terrifying children & disgracing
all of us / who can stand on our own two feet /
watching apartheid as if it were another all-night movie

Pages for a Friend

letters from friends used to be an art form
literary exquisite observations of the soul
aesthetics and compulsions to give
order to whatever this life is
pages for a friend kept many a prairie
woman / lingering by her fire in a sod house
from committing suicide / some prairie
women killed themselves anyway
the letters from their friends

crushed in their fists / the same
fists that beat walls trying to
keep up enough anger not to die
not to burn the kettle swinging

over the fire / the ladle too hot to handle
loneliness stalking the
        farmyard a warring Comanche

pages for a friend fluttering off
in the wind / lost breaths wishes
dying for someone to loom over the horizon
anyone / come talk / please come talk to me / now
i've no one to write
i'm so lonely i'm not sure i remember
how it is you read
you see i've memorized all the letters
my woman friends sent me
i could recite some to you
let me make some coffee &
we could sit & talk
please, mister, let's just talk
before i forget how & become silence.

Walk, Jump, Fly

mommy can i tell you something
mommy can i share you something
mommy can i tell you something
excuse me mommy can i share you something
mommy mommy would you watch me
mommy can you see me now
mommy can i tell you something
mommy we need to give jesus
something he's been in a cave three days
what should we get jesus / mommy
can i show you something / excuse me
mommy / nobody likes me at school /

mommy can i tell you something
mommy can i tell you something / we
have to get Donald Duck a birthday present /
he's fifty years old / mommy what do
you think Donald would like / mommy
can i tell you something / mommy

mommy mommy mommy

can i tell you something / i got
27 valentines / everybody at school loves
me / me / mommy can i tell you something
excuse me mommy can i show you something
mommy this is for you mommy open it
now / mommy do you like it / mommy
can i show you something / mommy
can i tell you something / these
are different flowers vases violets
& thistles / mommy did you know that /

mommy mommy mommy

mommy can i ask you something / please
mommy can i ask you something / mommy
do you love me / oh good i'm glad mommy
i love you mommy / mommy can i ask you something
mommy i just wanna ask you one more
thing / mommy can you fly?

Ntozake Shange, "The Vicki Series #1," Oil on Canvas,
24″ x 18″

"for Vickie Miller"

6-30-85
Rothko Chapel
Houston, Texas

I don't exactly know why out of all of us / all of us who knew & loved Vickie Miller / why i was chosen to speak as one voice for us all / one voice that desperately needs assuaging now / needs reassurance that we loved & gave as much to her as she gave to us.

Vickie & i did silly things / we dyed our hair purple one week / then blue the next week & spent the summer of '84 with lavender hair awaiting the arrival of Prince & Sting to carry us away from the loneliness of being single parents whose families were far off somewhere / families we could remember / but not depend on for immediate solace or relief from solitude & tea parties with imaginary friends.

We always spoke of husbands & fathers as the missing elements in our lives / not realizing that we were becoming one another's family / & that search for love & companionship is fraught with complexities, frustrations & passions that sometimes overwhelmed us & led us away from ourselves to the extent that someone else's needs pre-empted our own.

Once Vickie told me that her life was worthless, that she added nothing to the world, she wasn't an artist, she wasn't a doctor or an architect / she couldn't type & on & on she went / once more not realizing that she brought joy & mischief & love into ourselves / simply by being herself / her life was worth all that we feel now for her / no one shall take her place / i am praying that her spirit / her high-spirited reckless soul / hears us finally & rests knowing that we've gathered together in her name / because she was worth every second, every conversation / every night at Rich's / every birthday party & quiet afternoon over champagne or tea / she was worth each telephone call we made asking for her and her compassion / she was part of our family / blood lines superceded by her generosity, forthrightness & that peculiar giggle of hers / see, Vickie / we're all here tonight because you held a special place in each one of our lives / you always will be in our lives / & that's not just worthwhile, Vickie, that's because we love you.

Please take a moment of silence now / & we shall let Vickie's spirit pass over each one of us / very much the way she passed thru our lives to the other side. Lord, be a witness to our testimony / may Vickie Miller find peace with you / may hell be the lot of the one who stole her from us. we shall not forget. I shall not forgive as God is my witness.

Donna Henes, "Wrapping the Wind/Spider Woman Series," Fluorescent Flagging, Montauk Pt., N.Y.

Wrapping the Wind

Candlemass 1980

the waves leave the dunes sculpted
momentarily heaving & shifting
sand across the paths the
waves thrash / catch it
seize it / the wind leaves signs
we can read the future
sand drawings
sand prints / signals of ancient
ways / wrap the wind in
beautiful colors / flow like the sea
lie naked in the face of the moon
her tides / rocked to sleep
by the crocheted wisps of
wind / the kind that makes your
cheeks tingle / & humility that makes
us cry / once we've known the
wind / a fleeting lover / caressing our
souls / wrap the wind / & hold it tight.

Cocoon Ceremony

Lake Margarethe, Michigan

wrap me in the waters
in the silken lilting waters
fresh flowers floating by my bosom
down creeping along my arms
searching for my wings
wrapped in waters & new spun
wool / i am a mariposa
disguised as a woman
unwind the yarns my threads
colored rust & twilight
discover the mysteries
the delight of women water
& air / breathe life slowly
papillon / know your delicacy
dare to betray mine & i become
a black snake / winding slinking
knowing my enemy.

Dressing Our Wounds in Warm Clothes

we're as fragile as slight tree limbs
laden with ice on a fierce winter day
we lay up by the escalator in Penn Station
eating our cures & way / our tuna in cans
our clothes in a shopping cart from
somewhere / the big apple store / not
Balducci's or the Jefferson Market
we wear three & four dresses at a time
walk barefoot down 8th avenue
we have sometimes a peculiar odor
but no worse from the women's room
at Penn Station / people carry
suitcases & travel bags / take trains
go places / they're sturdy & mindful
this spot / our rags protect us
see i designed this myself / no one
anywhere looks quite like this
is my beauty.

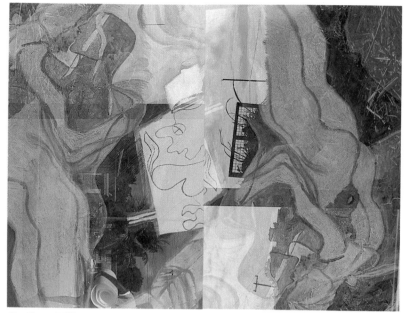

Candace Hill-Montgomery, "Glimmering Through the African Brush," mixed media, 17″ x 14″ each panel

La Luta Continua

The sunlight hit Jean-René. The sepia half-moon of a mole by his right cheekbone glistened, steaming coal in a fast car gliding through the hills of Morocco. We stopped to have a very French picnic: kisses. Shadows of lips and teeth against luxurious auburn soil. The sun always slipping in and out of the bends of limbs, wine from Lisbon dancing mouth to mouth, tongues tracing patterns of clouds, scents of goats, sheep, and the last of my Opium, somewhere near Meknes. I wanted to stay in Paris I'd thought, but no. He said he'd have to have me somewhere I'd never been. I'd laughed. I woke in Casablanca to morning prayers and croissants.

If only my mother could see me now: Jean-René meticulously placing strawberries, blueberries, kiwi, grapes, melon balls, in a crescent round my vulva. Oh dear. Oh dear. Oh dear. My cat has yellow eyes. Now my pussy has lime green ones, amber pupils, slits.

Casablanca was hot, noisy, trashy, roadblocks everywhere, the war in Spanish Sahara. We retreated like Anaïs to the countryside. This Guadalupan velvet spur of a man and me, Liliane. I travel a lot. I look at men and take some home or leave the country, borders have never intimidated me. My passport is in order and I carry letters of credit, perfume, four fancy dresses, and six nightgowns. I always sleep naked alone at least once a week. I pray and say Hail Marys by some window at dusk. It's always best for me to deal with the sacred when I'm naked. For me it has something to do with humility.

I found Jean-René at the fast-food place eating souvlaki next to the Moulin Rouge. I was flirting with some Brazilians from the Folies Bergères. I'd just left Lisbon and Angola was on all our minds.

In my last paintings, before I left New York, I superimposed AK-47s over fetal transparencies under Frelimo banners. *La Luta Continua* was the name of the show. There was no way to stop my fingers, my arms, I was jumping up and down ladders to get the touches of blood and fresh corpses finely detailed so there'd be no doubt that the Portuguese left a country the way vampires leave blond white women: drained of life and scarred. I paint. I don't talk too much. The world overwhelms me. I can give up what I see. I see a lot. I believe in honor, color, and good sex.

Machado and Axel from the Folies were doing their best to entice me to La Plantation, an Antillean discothèque near St. Germaine des Prés. I looked Jean-René in the eyes once, and knew that would never happen. Why would I want to dance in a plantation anyway? Even in the presence of the singularly defined muscles of Latin dancers, one on either side, the man I was slowly seducing across the room just kept looking at me, knowing where I'd be going. I like that. I like a man to know what the deal is going to be in an instinctive, absolute, lyrically facile manner. I like a man with confidence. Take me from these two sweet mutha-fuckahs simply by looking. Do that and I'll be gone. Wherever we are going. I mean, if a man's up to that. I love double entendres, double negatives, duels. Some cocks have triggers; others are freckled or uncircumcised.

I decided I wanted some baklava. Right over there where the man with eyes was sucking me up. Imagine that, disappearing into a stranger's eyes in Paris. How would they find me? Who would know to look? I don't leave any tracks, am quick to burn bridges. My friends, well my friends, the real ones, wouldn't think twice. Liliane's, she's having dessert. They'd smile, unless no drawings arrived in say a month or two. That is my signature, after all, an image. I forget what I was wearing that night. Probably the floor-length azure crepe with lace triangles up to my hips and no back at all. I like that dress, but I'm going to dye it *grise: ma robe grise.* Oh, Jean-René slid his eyes into my mouth and asked me if I had plans for the evening. "Mais non, Monsieur, j'ai pensé que tu voudrais faire des arrangements." I told him my name several hours later. By then he could barely speak.

Jean-René with the black nipples that grew. Each tongue flick drawing licorice sticks tiptoeing over my teeth and tongue. Third-world delicacies. Cascades of caviar round my neck. *Noire et blanche.* He played the piano, when he wasn't near me. Actually he was a concert pianist. He played Bach and Stravinsky, when he wasn't near me. He sometimes played scales, but anybody can do that.

Coming down the Champs Élysées all the record stores blasted Stevie Wonder's newest release, *Songs in the Key of Life.* "Isn't She Lovely" chased me from corner to corner. I didn't know if I should hide near the gated windows or fly through the night like some paradisiacal bird of color: many colors. Any color, everything matches: spirit; free spirits; about to be in love a lot. Stevie Wonder pushing us closer together. Eventually, I stopped running. I walked fast. Waited by the curb. At some point he put his arm over my bare shoulder. His fingers grasped my skin so there were five imprints. A woman with three sets of fingerprints. That would drive Interpol crazy. I was already grazing the edges. I didn't leave his side till we got to where we began. Remember the hillside outside Meknes? You won't believe me, but I heard Charlie Palmieri in Paris on our way to heaven. Those fingers again. I'll have to draw it for you, okay?

Such character you'd expect from C.T.'s, Cecil Taylor's, fingers or my grandfather's, Frank, who was a master carpenter. My fingers still smack of perfumed talcum, white gloves, and honied lotions. My calluses are elusive, if ever present, closer to my heart than my wrists, which are deceitfully delicate. Veins, blue-black pulsing, rise eloquently from Jean-René's hands, small muscles throb over the white and black keyboard, eliciting the reveries of Bartók, Monk, Abrams, and Joplin. My back refused to sound anyone but Satie, Bobby Timmons, and John Hicks. This frustrates Jean-René. When he smacks my cheek with the back of his hand, only Andrew Cyrille comes to mind. The Frenchman is unnerved. The music of my body is deliberate. There's nothing I can do about how I sound. When I open my mouth, Shirley Cesaire and Jeanne Lee scramble for the skies, my tongue finds his somewhere high above the treble clef. We're pulled back, flat to the soils. Sun running us *pianissimo* while our sweat moistens the virginal African grass. Our bodies lay claim to the earth, silhouettes of lovers, smooth unbroken lines, enveloped by tall brush, quivering in the wind, as tongues would wag in whatever language were our license with each other known beyond this side of the road. Meknes.

I want to paint now. Throw Jean-René's swarthy limbs over the pillows I laced with scents of raspberry, bay leaves, cinnamon. He'll rest in soft fragrances: me and my spices. I pull out my brushes and pastels. Sequester myself on a rocky cliff before the walled village. Women wrapped in blue-black swishes of spun cotton float through the streets. The men in white and tanned robes saunter with a holy gait toward a precipice. It is dusk. I am using wine as water to moisten my paints. The air is too light for oils. Watercolors, moistened pastels alone, capture the haunting prayers of these disciples of Allah. I am allowing my fingers to float as the women do, over the cobblestones, reddened dirt paths, billows of dust following donkeys, mules, bicycles. My brush strokes un-evenly. The abyss around which we assemble in honor of Allah. The evening prayers begin. The sun splits open, cries for atonement and adoration pierce the clouds, hovering weights above our heads. I feel a sharp pain in my groin, my heart is racing, I am losing my breath. I see Jean-René. His eyes are glazed over as if in a trance. I swoon. My blood has come. The forces of this sacred earth have drawn menses from my body. The sun sets. I use this last scarlet liquid to highlight the figures in my painting. Hundreds of women, floating blue-black apparitions etched *rouge,* the soil *rouge,* the brush-colored caftans of the men dragging in blood. The Jihad has simple implications. Holy War. Where is there war without blood. Blood falling to the ground. I am weak now. I leave my paints and brushes alone, slide over to Jean-René, who holds me close to him as if we'd been in danger, as if communion with God was a travesty. We can't kiss, not now. Fierce angels are everywhere, sneering and eager to mock our frailties. Mortals, flesh, driven souls, seeking wholeness with mouths, fingers, wrapping limb over limb to become one. Music issuing forth from their depths, entering one another, desperately seeking that one song, one melody of peace. The angels gather above the rushes, snide, shaking their heads, wagging their fingers through the air, lighting up the sky and calling thunderous rhythms to startle us, to insist we acknowledge our nakedness. I pull my paintings to me. The colors pour onto my skin. I am now streaked blue-black, reds, yellow, luminous blue. Jean-René grabs my hand. I hold my paintings, soaking in the downpour. Scarlet drops fall from my bosom to my toes, to the soil, blue-black smudges crowd off my own sepia tones. Lurching toward the car, I turn. Drop the paintings. Fall on my knees, bleeding. Pleading with Allah to bless me, to accept me as an instrument of the holy spirit. Jean-René whispers Hail Marys in my ears. I am digging for the scent of my god. My hands are covered with small rocks, brown mud and slivers of brush, up to my wrists where the clay has dried like bracelets. Jean-René lifts me in one movement, holding me a statue over the ruins of my art.

My hands were small fists, knotted round the earth I'd gathered. Jean-René glanced at me once. "We're going to Fez. If you want to save that dirt, there's a small box in the back. Wipe the blood from your arms and face or we'll never get a hotel room." My eyes followed the rise of his cheekbones, the arrogance of his slender nose, and the flippant curve of his lips, those finely wrought muscles in his forearm. Yes, the box, save the soil for earth paintings. Wipe the blood away. Watch Jean-René take the road, soaring, an ebony eagle, round mimosa and hibiscus and palms. Jean-René smoldering like Mont St. Pierre, but this volcano was holding the eruption for me. The woman shedding blood and soil in the back seat of an Antillean eagle's flight to Fez.

I liked to kiss Jean-René on curves or steep downhill glides. I liked the wandering tree limbs to let their shadows enter his mouth as my tongue did. Shadows and tongue skipping and sliding over his pearl teeth and blackberry lips. Dangerous, you say? *Mais non.* You're talking to the woman who was physically searched three times at Kennedy Airport because the buzzer went off whenever I went through the screening device. I had forgotten to take my ben-wa balls out. They're no threat to international security. When they're working, the last thought on my mind is hijacking a plane. Why should I swipe an airplane when young Guadeloupean peacocks stalk about Paris and fly me to Morocco in the middle of the night. All he needs is a piano and me. I carry my own entertainment: color, wine, brushes, pencils. My ben-wa balls attracted no attention at Orly Airport. I guess they could see the contentment of my face, or smell my pleasure. I always assume people can smell how happy I am, how full of love I can be. That's how Jean-René found me in Paris at that fast-food souvlaki place. He could smell my joy, he said. I told him I heard Eric Dolphy in his eyes.

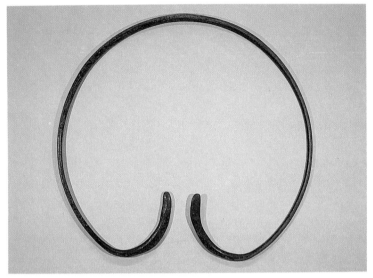

Martin Puryear, "Dream of Pairing," Painted Wood, 51½" x 54½" x 2"

Dream of Pairing

i dream of coupling
discovering the stranger who'd be one with me
i dream all night long of this man
his face changes but is always full of love
for me / sometimes i manage to hold his hand
once we danced at Xenon's to LaBelle
but it might have been the Jacksons
he threw me over his head & drew
me tween his legs like those old
WWII jitter buggers / the way George
Faison did at Magique on Motown's 25th
anniversary party / i've never let
him kiss me / he wanted to / this stranger
who visits me in my dreams / but that
would be too personal / he's never
told me his name.

Tango

loose in the brush pines
my grandfather farmed
learned yiddish to better wash windows
the french windows
the sixteen paned windows
the terraced windows
of a restricted town
he made violins of pine
varnished them tuned them
let music carry his daughters
out of the town
away from the farm that
burned down
scrubby pines brush pines
obliterate the ruins of the barn
the pine needles scratch the air
each time my father wipes the
tears from his cheeks
but not from the windows
there were never streaks
on the windows.

Box & Pole

we must make totems
how else can the spirits feel us
how else can they know we must reach
for them in ourselves / our spirits
roam the skies the soil & the seas
not unlike other deities / we require
homage sacrifice & offerings
those things we must give ourselves
aztecs dressed in the skins of the dead
yorubans deliver yemaya white blossoms
& champagne / incas offered gold
& coca leaves / we must build totems
for the spirits / we must worship ourselves
that the earth not be defiled
by our neglect / our ignorance of ritual
after all the universe has given us
the seasons / the warmth of loving.

Where the Heart Is

i need me a house like that
a small mansion i could see through
from every angle / with one door only
i could enter / i could let my mind
be that / a small castle i could
lock myself in when the world's
too big ferocious and static fulla
things i just cant understand
but my mind is packed with trunks
of memories closets fulla fears /
stairways that lead me to scars
i hate in myself / i need me a
house like that one / a bungalow
by the sea, "where the heart is"
where i can love myself in an empty
space / & maybe fill it with kisses.

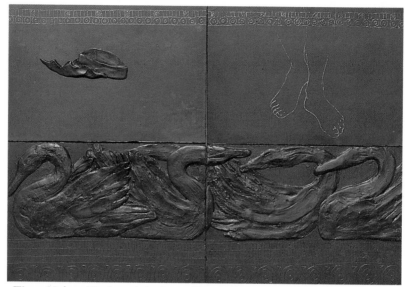

Wopo Holup, "Leda and the Swan," Bas-relief, sealed cement, 24″ x 34″ x 2″

between the two of them

it musta happened to you/ it
couldn't just be me/ who got her head turned
by a bird/ not an ordinary pigeon/ hangs out
near Grand Central/ or some cock parading
past Three Roses/ but a plush ol'
son of a gun/ justa glidin' through the water
leanin' his head from left to right/
Cab Calloway in slow motion/ with
eyes gazin' blasphemous right thru to my G-spot.
you musta run across this fella
my husband claims he never saw him/
but I wanna tell you/ messin' with
that creature made me wish/ I had
wings/ so I could catch up to where &
how & ooooh/ was I flyin'.

Patrice Viles, "The Wedding," Necklace

Twanda B. Johnson's Wedding

I married myself today in front of the $6,000 opal next to the $4,000 aquamarine from Brazil where I seduced a taxi driver for the sheer pleasure of such gloriously full lips, licking my forehead at the red lights, long black curls seeping through my individually applied aqua blue super long lashes: dew in a tropical place. I was a scented collection of crystal sweat from my elbows to my chin. My legs sweating so. While my vulva trembled, dripping woman all over the backseat. Sweet years ago with the Cariocas.

Beverly wanted the man to drive us home. I told her that was exactly what he was doing. My mouth murmured, filled with lip, tongue, moustache. Oh, moustache massaging the corners of my lips, tickling the crevice tween my ears and hair falling over the front seat. "For God sake, let the man drive us to the hotel," Beverly screamed. I know she did, but the kisses were synchronized to the yellow and red lights from Corcuvado to Leme. There was so much of Rio we hadn't seen. She should lay back with some cachaca and sight-see or huddle up, take a little nap. But definitely forget the notion that the kisses could be stopped by dawn or high noon, lest we fell asleep tongue to tongue somewhere near the sailboats headed toward Itaparica. I forget his name, but that's how you should be kissed when the minister proclaims "you are now man & wife."

I'm going to get a veil to wear to the jewelry store and carry my Sony Walkman behind my bouquet, listening to Prince croon "you, you I would die for you." Then I'd slip the wedding ring over the wrong finger: the independent second finger right near the real wedding finger. After all, this friend of mine told me if the so-called wrong finger was manicured and long, there was no mistaking what all he could bring out of you, anywhere. The wrong finger was a telling sign of incurable delights, up & over labia, vulva, clitoral sambas, etc.

I sang to myself à la Irene Cara and Natalie Wood, "There's a place for us." And asked the price of the Swiss digital watch embraced by diamonds and sapphires: 8,556 American dollars. Nicaraguan currency was not negotiable. Cuban pesos by the thousands totally unacceptable. So, I couldn't give that sparkling glinting tease of a time keeper to myself as an engagement present. I had missed my engagement party cause I had impulsively accepted my hand in marriage without so much as calling my mother. I hadn't even visited my Dad to ask for my hand, nor had I listened to what he expected from me as my life-long partner: the man to take Daddy's place in my life, choosing and buying my silk dresses and lightly salted sweet butter at the few Weingartens left in Texas. Nothing takes the place of Jamail's, but my Dad couldn't know that. He's not intimately familiar with Houstonian traditions or fads. Why, his cowboy hat doesn't even have feathers on it and his boots got that thin "eastern" leather that would surely tear if you were steel-dogging or barrel-racing.

We didn't have the conversation.

I continued the marital ceremony over malachite and Australian opals that have black and navy hints amidst azure, pale green and coral rose swirls ensconced in gold where my Maid of Honor would have held my fiancé's ring for that sacred moment, the exchanging of rings. Giving oneself to another in the view of the Holy Ghost, through the haunting chime of the Sikh's gong, with the blessings of Ochun and Shango, never far from the reach of Élegua or Ogun and Krishna, the Breath of Fire ridding my soul and flesh of the now inconsequential past, pushing me toward purity and passion and innocence. My mate familiar with my blazing uncontrollable untouched bronze rose longings/ knowing, never having caressed me, where I might sigh, close my eyes humbly accepting more palm, right there/ more thigh/ more thigh over here. Please, listen. To marry oneself surrounded by semi-precious stones and crystal is quite an experience.

If one's ballet dancer is somewhere in Latin America, rehearsing blocking for "Swan Lake" or "Fix Me, Jesus, Fix

Me," a gift from Ailey to Pinochet in memory of Allende to the repertory company at the Teatro Municipal in Santiago/ out of Santiago/ in Bogotá/ on to Caracas/ el Districto Federal, where I shall honeymoon at the Maria-Isabel, drink margaritas in sight of Our Lady of Guadalupe. Shall I make my pilgrimage on my knees with the shrouded *Indias,* approaching our Holy Mother? Shall I execute triplets and piqué turns to our healer, our conduit to Christ, while the dancer goes on to Guadalajara?

I am marrying myself under a new moon in East Texas: care-taker, provider, disciplinarian, the only alternative, still smelling of Opium, magnolia incense. My ring's on the wrong finger in this, the last days of the twentieth century. I shall have been a wife for 14 years by the year 2000, breeding poems, novels, a graceful clarity to my people in the New World where all things are possible. I dont know my campañero yet, but when he finds me I'll be certain to look him directly in the eye to see courage, see fearlessness and honor in the carriage of his torso. Legs revealing deft continuous preparation for an assault contra nuestra dignidad y liberación. Cultural aggression skipping to Uxmal, Machu Picchu, the Pyramid of the Moon. My lover and I shall seek out Curanduras and Padrinos to put us in touch with mountain cloud river soil. The wedding ceremony was very simple, wasn't mentioned in the *Enquirer* or the *New York Times* society pages. The *San Juan Star* ran a five-line announcement. *Jet* magazine edited our union out of "People Are Talking About" to *Ebony*'s fashion section, since my dress was designed by Beverly Parks of Miami, who had studied with Valentino. After all, they had to acknowledge that my flower girl wore a Norma Kamali mid-calf satin gown, while I paraded around the $10,000 bracelets and earrings, as if I were wearing them all under a raw silk canopy studded with aging ivory tusks, fading from opaque white toward fawn rippling spirals tween boars' teeth, Chinese monkeys of silver and carnelian, jade beads swinging from one lapis oval to another, a loop of garnets in semicircles enclosing my bridal carriage, enveloped with Uzi machine guns and 367. Magnums at each corner. Bands of ammunitions lay across the palominos' backs, slowly tracing the paths of Guillén and Neruda, sidling up to Marquez and Galisch. At Casa de las Américas the entire wedding party was treated to mohitos.

We moved on to the silver services: punch bowls, champagne glasses. They do not carry sterling silver machetes or gold Galils. But these things may be ordered, if I would sign the wedding book near the Chippendale parlor chair which is not for sale. I really hadn't intended to have so grand a ceremony that *Jeune Afrique* carried a two-page feature in their August issue. *Marie-Claire* and *Elle* critiqued the designers of all the bridesmaids' dresses. I hate symmetry. Nothing in nature is symmetrical. So, how could I marry myself surrounded by a slew of bridesmaids in the same color with peau de soie heels dyed somewhere near 42nd Street and 9th Avenue. I couldn't bear it. My gorgeous friends appeared as themselves near the crystal wine glasses and delicate liqueur sets which could be monogrammed, if I knew my husband's name, which I did, of course, since it was me. But I didn't want to upset the saleswoman, who didn't realize she was the only woman in America with an eight-inch-high bleached honey blond beehive and a circle pin on the left lapel of her mauve two-paneled jacket. I just said my husband's name was Johnson, so a "J" would do on the liqueur glasses, but the water, champagne, wine, and brandy glasses were to remain clear of design or inscription of any kind. Who knows? Some guerrillero from Guatemala or Namibia might find me irresistible, put the rings on the right wedding finger. Have a last name that began with "X" like Xiomaro, or "V" like Valenzuela, or even "M" like Malinké. Something told me my marriage to myself would end gracefully, but would certainly not be the last venture to the guarded fears and hopes of another whose very name drew tears on occasion, whose acerbic temper cut sinews, breastplate, clammy hands, trembling fingers, only to elicit the aching pain of truth. One cannot marry and lie. A lot of people will testify to that. Tween husband and wife is a ravine where spring water finds its way to the creek, then to the river/

where silt and aluminum cans infect the coming together of disparate currents, leaving swamps and signs reading "this water unfit for bathers." And who are bathers but lovers chastened with sacred drops of pungent perspiration and milk sweet white water crests racing to ankles, roaming toes irrigating the very soils where spirits seek ambrosia.

I've been here a long time. I am almost joined to myself, "in sickness and health, for richer or poorer, till death do we part." But I've got to get over to I-10 to the gun store. I did promise my fiancé a gilded silver antique zip-gun that was actually used by the Blackstone Rangers. I had asked for a black leather jacket, the kind the Savage Skulls wear on the East Side train: silver studs on the sleeves and round the waist. Very hard to come by. They are passed down in families. And my family left the Bronx as the War in Europe was ending, before Hiroshima or the Bandung Conference, before I was born. So I agreed to settle for one of Ben Webster's mouthpieces or a Jimi Hendrix diary.

The yellow beehive lady caught on that I was not a regular customer. I might be a single black mother, you know, a statistic. But she was wrong. I simply got married, swathed in cascades of nature's rugged rocks refined by human hands to steal the sunlight, shake the moon from her sleep, and let the world know I am well taken care of. Diamonds, emeralds, silencers, rapid-fire machine guns, poetry, Dom Perignon, camouflage suits, gold lamé high-top sneakers, mindful we must be twice what we believe we are, two times more than expected, I'm so literal I had to get married to get two of me.

But we're joined: a union of two minds, two spirits/ two believers in la revolución/ not even a free trip on the Concorde could pull us apart.

I heard a Nicaraguan, only 18 years old, and in the militia, jokingly reply to a possible chabala: "But you know I can't marry you, I'm married to the Revolution." You better be careful, she's jealous, and never loses. She loves to dance. See you at Rich's Thursday. We'll bring the struggle to every nightclub in Houston. Come on, why stay fighting for truth and commitment, if your compañero (lover-male) or compañera (lover-female) can't dance. No one has ever said a bomba was counter-revolutionary or that break-dancing was an anarchist distraction. My lover, also known as La Victoria, chose the wrong finger for the rings, but gave me lessons I'll never forget. I am like you the strength of two, la lucha y la cultura. The D.C. Bop and a shotgun. Siempre, our spouse calls out: "La lucha continuá." We dance by the sea between the land mines. When I married myself among the jewels of our planet, my husband taught me to aim accurately, to never weaken, and never, no matter what, never forget we fight for love, por amor y la luna; for the future, y nuestra derecho; to know how to read; to have a pair of shoes; to watch our children grow, not dying flaccid in our arms, pus oozing from their miniature limbs. We fight for love.

If you married la lucha by yourself like I did, we can dance all night & wake facing our beloved, La Victoria. We can't put the rings on the wedding finger till the earth's jewels swing a treacherous merengue from the hips of our children and whip like braided rawhide the columns of the courthouses where we are tortured and made ugly, when we know every scar is a beauty mark.

The beehive lady is dimming the lights in her gilded room. She's walking me to the door, not knowing that next time I shall bring a brigade of unwed mothers who will marry themselves, however they please. We're our own electricity, lady. These lights wont dim till nuestras compañeros come racing through Hermann Park, embracing the women who knew so well what they wanted. She married herself. Her hands moving with his to shout or caress by bougainvillea, always close to the soil. He or she moves the wedding band and the engagement ring to the right finger. La Victoria is not common. I don't stray from my old man, though he's not around much. I can feel his feet trudging those mountains, feel his breath searching my cheeks, my neck, for a sign that I am there. Yes, kisses by the glass doors just as the iron gates slam shut. Kisses that make me shake till I scream out for more, por amor, amante. We must be two for every one of them. We are the jewels of the New World, hard & sensual. Our romance is tough like *la guitarra armada*. A loaded fast dance. Hey, look, every woman in the IRT is trying to catch the bouquet I bought myself when I changed from the Flushing Line to the A train. It's on you, honey. You got to be all you can or you'll find yourself standing at some altar all by yourself, trying to imagine why the rest of you is sauntering down Westheimer looking for a precious stone without an appropriate setting: some jewel mistaking herself for rhinestones. Damn, I only have fifteen minutes to get to the gun store. Oh, I hope they are not out of those silver zip guns. The ballet dancer is still in Buenos Aires. The taxi driver in Rio doesn't even know I've gotten married. Now I know for a fact that he is a fascist. None of that will do me any good, if I try to carry myself up the stairs. I'ma do a time step like the Nicholas Brothers. No one will know the difference. I mean, do I look married to you?

Robert Mapplethorpe, "Untitled," Photograph: Vibert Williams, 1984

irrepressibly bronze,
beautiful & mine

I

all my life they've been near me
these men/
        some for a while like the
friend of my father's who drove
each summer from denver to
st. louis/with some different
white woman/i remember one seemed
to like me/she had rose blond hair
i wondered/why do you like me
you're with him & he's mine
he's colored/he'll always be
like that/like me/i think
he knew my eight-year-old
precocious soul was hankering
for days to come with one/
one of them colored fellas
who'd be mine/on purpose/not
just cause of some pigmentation
problem/or a grandfather clause
in mississippi/i lived there near
the water/the river/the silt
caking my calves/me laughin with
the younguns/the boys who'd be
black men one day
                    if they lived so long

he brought me rocks/each sojourn
quartz marble granite & sandstone
onyx ovals i could hold onto when
he drove off with the white woman
i never felt sad/i didn't know i might

be experiencing rejection/a little
colored girl with an ebony stone
in the palm of her hand
i knew that was his heart

where could a man go without his heart
a child by the mississippi grasping
dreams/yet to grab holto a man
but nighttime & motown asked me to dance
sang sweet streams of sweat
moist kisses/those arrogant torsos
daring crackers or a fool to
look the wrong way/no just look
a funny way & it'd be over
or just begun

look at me pretty niggah

bring it over here/i'm grown
now & the stones don't sit
static in my hand/you know
how it is black volcanoes erupt
they say when miles davis manages
to whisper/they erupt they say
when the blackstone rangers take
a stroll/black volcanoes seep
lava anywhere there's true love
now i'm not talkin about
a hoot and holler or a dance on a dime
but whenever there's true
love/black volcanoes seep lava
& it's always been mine
always my dear like the Bible
says an eye for an eye/there's
a me for a you

bring it on baby

i've been holding your heart in
my hand since i was a child
i've been preoccupied on occasion
        but i had to grow some too
cause i wanted what all you were
what all you are/now you're a man
you've got the world watchin your
every move/i've got your heart
& by the mississippi/when i was a
        child/we callt that a groove
sweet black-eyed pea
honey dripped husk

        bring it on/i'm not afraid

i've known you all my life
        & this my dear is just the
beginning
the first inkling of what they're gonna
        hear
it ain't no lie that we could sing
don't be embarrassed/just appear
right there
        the way i have you/those
times you're brown & wet/those
times your strength can't be met
just be
        &
remember me/oh back then
when you rode off & left
        your heart in the palm
        of my child hand

                II
he's of course george jackson
doing push-ups and visiting with angela

soledad   soledad

confined to his beauty alone
fighting cement walls for air
malcolm's last breath king's crumbling torso
speak to me of beauty
blood beauty courage sweating rage
of course he's lumumba
see only the eyes/bob marley wail
in the night ralph featherstone
burning temples as pages of books
become ashen and smolder by his ankles
walter rodney's blood fresh soakin
the streets/léon damas spoke poems
with this face/césaire cursed our
enemies/making welcome our true voice
the visage of a people
continually mourning
recognized our beauty so slowly
our heroes fade like jackie wilson
in silence/in the still of the night

soledad mi amor soledad

III

among palms whistling lizards
nestle by roots freshly humid
roots by palm fronds the sun
tickles lovers inviting them to
make quickly some love in
moist sands seeping through toes
pull down the bosom the legs
wiry & thick haired pull down
the petticoats/lace panties
perfumed lips skipping over
shoulders muscles making music
where before only acacias & macaws
dared solo/many duets

have been abandoned by the trunks
of palms searching for
moonlight/rushing toward the sky
as tongues would wrap round
each other/dew like honey
slipping from their lips
whole skies fallen by
their feet/

    jaguars prowl when their
eyes meet.

Jules T. Allen, "New Orleans Nuptials," Photograph

new orleans nuptials

i knew i'd know the ends of the earth
    before you'd have me fully
i'd prowl chichén itzá in a pick-up truck/
    take three steps/ three flaps/ three slaps
ku-dapi flap chassé/ assemblée
wings of an imperial moth fluttering over your tongue

you/
you could have me no other way/ than
all at once
the sun never sets/ i lay naked
at dawn/ at dusk
a nutmeg nude blues to a heaving tempting *soleil*
spraying/ blaring deserts
cross my thighs my breast my heart
longing for lips no longer familiar with other labia
than mine

all fruits plucked above/ below & around
the circumference of the earth/ now me
the equator must now be my waist/ hiding innocence
among clouds/ the snows of mt. mckinley
cleansing me/ hardening/ making numb memories
of any other than me

at the circle hot springs i come alive
leap wildly round your whiskers/ breaking away
skittish sorrel wrestling with the bit/ of your choosing

you'd have to have me this way
brandied & apache in white leather by *la coupole*

i read voraciously of men/ who travel woman to woman
not mile by mile/ love by love
men who so entangle themselves with smells/
however we present ourselves/
lapis chins dusted clay polished marble beaten brush waxed
cherrywood hand painted tiles of arbitrary shapes/
hexagonal limbs wound round your chest/ spirals of fingers
rubbing your neck/ let me bask at midnight in sunlight
so slick you take me almost wholly in the glimmer
        of the birch
cottonwoods rustle like i am breathing
no other way than all/ (i must ferret out triplets halves
            quarters eighths sixteenths elevenths
                thirteenths/
any possibilities of divisions)

i knew i'd know the ends of the earth
        before you'd have me fully
above all/ above the mountains
coral roses bloom from the corners of my mouth/
salmon rush ferociously/ throwin themselves thru the arc
        of our bellies
more rushes of clear waters seep tween our thighs/
my calves search out brooks streams coves of you
        to swathe me
blue tortillas imagine themselves placenta/ over & over
i am growing/ my hair follows the horizons
carving my visions like mahogany bamboo cedar/ skeins
of sheepskin moss jalapeñas envelop my temples

from the ends of the earth i've come back to have you
as no one has had me before/

speak any language/ i'll know what you mean
look somewhere/ i'll see what you see
hold me/ let me kiss you
now/ we approach heaven

The Artists: Biographical Sketches

LAURA CAGHAN, an artist and designer with work in numerous private and corporate collections, recently moved from Houston to Huntington Beach, California. "My concerns have centered around two issues. First is the importance of trusting one's inner self, of listening with the heart. My second interest is paradox. *Night Lightning* is one in a series of volcano images exploring emotions held within and the contradiction between outer calm and inner fire."

PATRICIA OLLISON JERROLS (ONITA), born in San Antonio "with a cowboy for a father," was introduced to photography as a child by her brother Jerome and subsequently studied at the New York School of Photography. "My greatest thrill is photographing female artists during their fantasies for their next work."

ARTURO LINDSAY, former director of the Midtown Art Center in Houston, is an Afro-Panamanian visual artist whose work has been exhibited extensively in the Northeast, Texas, and Panama.

HOWARDENA PINDELL lives and works in New York City, teaches at the State University of New York at Stony Brook, attended Boston University and Yale (MFA), and was a curator at the Museum of Modern Art in New York, in the department of Prints and Illustrated Books.

ANITA STECKEL received the NEA for painting 1983–84. Her work has been exhibited internationally, including at the Whitney and Brooklyn Museums, Bienale (Medellin, Colombia), and Document a 7 (Germany). She teaches in New York City at The Art Students League and at Parsons School of Art.

HOUSTON CONWILL is a cultural worker residing in NYC with his wife, Kinshasha Holman Conwill. He attended Howard University and USC (MFA) and was the recipient of a Prix de Rome fellowship, a Guggenheim fellowship, and a New York Foundation for the Arts fellowship. He is the author of *F.U.N.K. HUMANIFESTO 2000 A.D.: The Funk Cosmology*.

LINDA GRAETZ was born in Omaha, studied art at the State University of New York at Stony Brook, Brandeis, the Museum of Fine Arts (Houston), and graduated from Clark University. Her works appear in collections throughout the U.S. (representation: Harris Gallery, Houston). Her musical and theatrical talents have been displayed in recent productions for the Museum of Modern Art in New York and New Music America. "I have lived in Texas for thirteen years. It is here that my passions for art, for nature (especially birds and the western landscape), and for freedom have been nurtured and allowed to thrive."

DONNA HENES is a ritual artist and urban shaman who has exhibited and performed across the U.S. and in Canada, England, Holland, Denmark, Italy, and Israel. An author and composer ("Chants for Peace★Chance for Peace," the first satellite peace message in space), she is co-founder of the International Center for Celebration and a book judge for the Jane Addams Peaceaward.

CANDACE HILL-MONTGOMERY is a visual artist using paint, photography, poetry, and other mediums to make visual books about perception. Her one-person shows include The New Museum of Contemporary Art, The Bronx Museum of the Arts, and, most recently, the Pentonville Gallery in London. She won a 1985–86 Guggenheim fellowship in visual art and a New York Foundation for the Arts fellowship in multi-media.

MARTIN PURYEAR was born in Washington, D.C., and lives and works in Chicago. He taught school in Sierra Leone,

West Africa, before doing graduate studies at the Swedish Royal Academy in Stockholm and at Yale University.

WOPO HOLUP was a Dr. Pepper Queen in Dallas in the late 1950s and now lives in New York City. The Ms. Holup and Ms. Shange team has taught at Sonoma State College, collaborated on two environmental art installations and two books of poetry, and currently has a third book of poetry in progress. She has had one-person exhibitions in New York and Chicago, and is a recipient of a CAPS fellowship, and NEA Artist-in-Residence and Con Edison grants.

PATRICE VILES was born in Vienna, has lived in Europe, Asia, and South America, attended art schools in Paris, San Francisco, and Dallas, and currently resides in Longview, Texas. She often uses European glass and metal from the 1930s and 1940s, and is exhibited in specialty stores and museum shops nationwide.

ROBERT MAPPLETHORPE has photographic works in dozens of permanent public collections, including the Australia National Gallery, Frankfurter Kunstverein, George Eastman House (Rochester, New York), Hara Museum of Contemporary Art (Tokyo), International Center of Photography (NYC), Israel Museum, Metropolitan Museum of Art, Museum of Fine Arts (Houston), Museum of Modern Art, Pompidou Center, San Francisco Museum of Modern Art, Stedelijk Museum (Amsterdam), and the Victoria and Albert Museum. *Black Book* is his eleventh and latest published collection.

JULES T. ALLEN is a photographer "apparently living and working" in New York City with a forthcoming book entitled *The Gym,* a study of Gleason's Gym, the legendary boxing facility. He has been awarded two CAPS fellowships from the New York State Council for the Arts.